Ten Po
about H

ex libris

Candlestick Press

Published by:
Candlestick Press,
Diversity House, 72 Nottingham Road, Arnold, Nottingham NG5 6LF
www.candlestickpress.co.uk

Design and typesetting by Diversity Creative Marketing Solutions Ltd.,
www.diversity.agency

Printed by Ratcliff & Roper Print Group, Nottinghamshire, UK

Selection and Introduction © Alison Brackenbury, 2019

Cover illustration © Lizzie Ginbey and Barry Tottle, 2019
www.inkyart.co.uk

Candlestick Press monogram © Barbara Shaw, 2008

© Candlestick Press, 2019
Reprinted 2021

Donation to Bransby Horses
www.bransbyhorses.co.uk

ISBN 978 1 907598 79 1

Acknowledgements:

The poems in this pamphlet are reprinted from the following books, all by
permission of the publishers listed unless stated otherwise. Every effort has been
made to trace the copyright holders of the poems published in this book. The
editor and publisher apologise if any material has been included without
permission or without the appropriate acknowledgement, and would be glad to be
told of anyone who has not been consulted.

Thanks are due to all the copyright holders cited below for their kind permission:

Alison Brackenbury, first published in this pamphlet. Jane Commane, *Assembly
Lines* (Bloodaxe Books, 2017) www.bloodaxebooks.com. Tony Curtis, *Pony*,
illus. David Lilburn (Occasional Press, Co. Cork, 2013) by kind permission of the
author. Sally Goldsmith, *Are We There Yet?* (Smith|Doorstop, 2013). Jen Hadfield,
Nigh-No-Place (Bloodaxe Books, 2008) www.bloodaxebooks.com. Dorothy
Hewett, *Wheatlands*, with John Kinsella (Fremantle Arts Centre Press, 2000) by
kind permission of the Estate of Dorothy Hewett and HLA Management Pty Ltd.
Geoffrey Holloway, *The Collected Poems of Geoffrey Holloway* (Arrowhead
Press, 2007) © Patricia Pogson. Maxine Kumin, *Where I Live: New & Selected
Poems 1990-2010* (W. W. Norton & Co. 2011) Used by permission of W. W.
Norton & Company, Inc. All rights reserved. Robert Wrigley, *The Church of
Omnivorous Light: Selected Poems* (Bloodaxe Books, 2013).

All permissions cleared courtesy of Swift Permissions
(swiftpermissions@gmail.com).

Where poets are no longer living, their dates are given.

Contents

Page

Introduction   *Alison Brackenbury*   *5*

Thaw   *Sally Goldsmith*   *7*

Ye Wearie Wayfarer   *Adam Lindsay Gordon*   *8*

Rebuke   *Geoffrey Holloway*   *9*

Seven Horse Secrets   *Jane Commane*   *10*

The Last Horse   *Alison Brackenbury*   *11*

After Seven Photographic Portraits of a Grey Connemara Pony   *Tony Curtis*   *12*

Paternoster   *Jen Hadfield*   *13*

Winter Bale   *Robert Wrigley*   *14*

Amanda Dreams She Has Died and Gone to the Elysian Fields   *Maxine Kumin*   *15*

The Grey Pony   *Dorothy Hewett*   *16*

Introduction

"Mark my words, the horse will be back!" These hopeful words came from my husband's great-grandfather, a stately Victorian coachman, who lived to see the internal combustion engine displace his life's work. Here is the horse's poetic comeback: a herd of poems, safely stabled.

Between these covers, you will find horses who are at ease, who are hard-ridden, who inspire love, sorrow, and humour. After thirty-five years of owning – or being owned by – my loyal cobs, I particularly commend to you the poems which warmly describe how humans, across this globe, care for horses.

By a British field, Geoffrey Holloway finds himself firmly rebuked for his failure to bring an apple! In the USA, Robert Wrigley's stallion faces danger from an uninvited guest in his winter hay, but Maxine Kumin and her mare sit together, sharing their carrot in the morning sun. Through an Australian drought, Dorothy Hewett rides her farm pony, joyfully transformed by a visit to the farrier. Welcome to a world of horses!

And how many horses still live with us here, in Britain? Officially, one million. (Horses, too, have passports!) Horse charities estimate that there could be a million more, undocumented. Some of these, sadly, are at particular risk of cruelty or neglect. Like Dorothy Hewett, we need to look out for them. But while I rounded up these poems, I was delighted to find many by younger writers. The horse will be back? The stately old coachman was wrong. In pasture, and in poetry, the horse has never left.

Alison Brackenbury

Thaw

A field snapped with frost and stitched with brittle docks,
a metal gate where I hung, still, like the horses there –

the grey standing gentle over the bay mare, held
inside their listening; wick-wick of a pigeon,

the chat of a jackdaw flock. Each second was a frozen bead,
but lovely to the touch. Once, he barely whisked his tail;

I watched. Then shifting my weight against the gate,
both turned and the mare lifted, nut-bright, out of her dream

then came slowly, and again on, slowly; the sky stretched
drum-skin, the sun low and sucked to a thin sweet.

She looked to the grey as if to say, *should I?* and a man
came, walking his dog. The mare whickered. *Grand!*

said the man. *It is*, I said, some strange thing thawing,
and she brought me her breath, timid to my hand.

Sally Goldsmith

Ye Wearie Wayfarer

Fytte 1: By Wood and Wold

Lightly the breath of the spring wind blows,
      Though laden with faint perfume,
'Tis the fragrance rare that the bushman knows,
      The scent of the wattle bloom.
Two-thirds of our journey at least are done,
      Old horse! let us take a spell
In the shade from the glare of the noon-day sun,
      Thus far have we travell'd well;
Your bridle I'll slip, your saddle ungirth,
      And lay them beside this log,
For you'll roll in that track of reddish earth,
      And shake like a water-dog.

Adam Lindsay Gordon (1833 – 1870)

Rebuke

I am at the gate.

You stand etched in sunlight,
then slowly canter down;
wind ruffling the russet nap
of your coat, turning
your mane spiky.

What do you want?
Love or apples?

I stroke, you toss your head,
show half a lip, teeth.

Love, I have no apples.

You stretch, obstinate,
nip my shirt.

What's love
but a giver of apples?
your silence says.

Geoffrey Holloway (1918 – 1997)

Seven Horse Secrets

The horse's heart is a grand mansion of four piston-firing chambers.

A horse sees a world blurred in the two-tone flourish of the photo finish.

Look into the amber planet of a horse's eye and a refracted universe forms there.

Horses turn the turf of an ever-moving, never-quite-touched earth beneath their hooves.

Horses laugh at our expense; lips peeled, ivory-gravestone teeth bared, domino pieces unplaced.

Horses are melancholic humourists; they know of the pending darkness beyond the five-bar gate, beyond the green paddock. Hancock learned all he knew from horses.

Horses tramp the ancient treadmill of our whims, trot to our bidding, broken, bought and sold, but only ever possess themselves.

Jane Commane

Last Horse

(Woody – Would-Be-Good – aged thirty-one.
A beautiful mare, from whom we never bred.)

The last? You stare. Can it be true
although I flew each hilltop track
ignored my mattress, torn to springs,
smoothed new rugs down the mare's broad back

since cataracts brought slow, scared dark
I called the vets, stood stilled and hard.
I watched the warm tail I had brushed
crumple upon the concrete yard.

We had grown old so long. I mourned
not gallop, a forgotten flame,
but her close heat in freezing stalls,
her throaty calls when buckets came.

Then sickness gripped my guts and heart.
I lay down on my daughter's bed.
Between trot, canter, deep, dazed sleep
I found her lit field in my head.

Once from long rides where hot hills rolled
to sun's glare, she would drift away.
Now, tail a flare, a melt of gold
she moved to me as at first day.

Blessed by light, one quick shadow
danced skittish all around her. Whole,
red ears pricked, from that blazed meadow,
breath to my dark, she led her foal.

Alison Brackenbury

After Seven Photographic Portraits of a Grey Connemara Pony

You will know a pony by its ears:
    Listening out for weather forecasts and love songs.

By its mane:
    Tossed over its eyes like a witch's broom.

By its coat:
    Always buttoned up, tight-fitting, dusty and well-worn.

By its eyes:
    That look at you, then look at you again to take you in.

By its hooves:
    Made for dancing, and so are worn at the tips.

By its mouth:
    That loves to eat words given with pats of the hand.

By its nose:
    That knows you, and lifts the pony's head to let it know you're coming.

By its tail:
    That conducts the symphony of birdsong, lake-song, light-song
    That is the bog underfoot, here above the village of Roundstone.

Tony Curtis

Paternoster

(for A.B.J.)

Paternoster. Paternoster.
Hallowed be dy mane.
Dy kingdom come.
Dy draftwork be done.
Still plough the day
And give out daily bray
Though heart stiffen in the harness.
Then sleep hang harness with bearbells
And trot on bravely into sleep
Where the black and the bay
The sorrel and the grey
And foals and bearded wheat
Are waiting.
It is on earth as it is in heaven.
Drought, wildfire,
Wild asparagus, yellow flowers
On the flowering cactus.
Give our daily wheat, wet
Whiskers in the sonorous bucket.
Knead my heart, hardened daily.
Heal the hoofprint in my heart.
Give us our oats at bedtime
And in the night half-sleeping.
Paternoster. Paternoster.
Hallowed be dy hot mash.

Jen Hadfield

Winter Bale

Not a scent so much as a bouquet
of smells, that stable: old wood, horse flesh,
the round sweet buds of manure;
molasses, oats, leather, hay.

In the ancient bushel basket a nest
of twine, now the red taut plunk of it cut
from the bale, as puffed up
out of the flakes comes dust

from the fields a year before,
and a stiff, sleepy bull snake oozes
over the cold floor and into the stall
where the edgy stallion waits for hay.

Robert Wrigley

Amanda Dreams She Has Died and Gone to the Elysian Fields

This morning Amanda
lies down during breakfast.
The hay is hip high.
The sun sleeps on her back
as it did on the spine
of the dinosaur
the fossil bat
the first fish with feet
she was once.
A breeze fans
the deerflies from lighting.
Only a gaggle of gnats
housekeeps in her ears.
A hay plume sticks out of her mouth.

I come calling with a carrot
from which I have taken
the first bite.
She startles
she considers rising
but retracts the pistons
of her legs and accepts
as loose-lipped as a camel.

We sit together.
In this time and place
we are heart and bone.
For an hour
we are incorruptible.

Maxine Kumin (1925 – 2014)

The Grey Pony

I was walking over paddocks
opening gates and crossing dry creekbeds
leading the foundered pony to Dutchy Butlers

she had foundered in the wheatfield
neglected   her hoofs had grown
like curved Turkish slippers
she stumbled as she walked

when we came to the smithy
built into the shoulder of the granite hillside
she stood quietly while he held each hoof on his knee
rasping away to the roar of the forge
the flame blown high in the funneling wind off the gully

I rode her back over the paddocks
picking her way with her old cunning
between the roots the stones and the rabbit burrows
she sidled through the silver air
pretending to shy at shadows
each hair of her coat
standing upright with joy.

Dorothy Hewett (1923 – 2002)